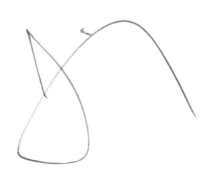

The Geography
of Feeling

Jimmy O'Connell

The Geography of Feeling

by Jimmy O'Connell

Copyright ©2023 Jimmy O'Connell

ALL RIGHTS RESERVED

ISBN 978-1-916620-31-5

Including the right of reproduction in whole
or in part in any form.

This edition printed and bound in the Republic of Ireland by

lettertec

Lettertec Publishing

Springhill House,

Carrigtwohill

Co. Cork

Republic of Ireland

www.selfpublishbooks.ie

Cover photography courtesy Diane Williams

ABOUT THE AUTHOR

Jimmy O'Connell was born in Dublin. He is a graduate of
U.C.D. He has been writing and performing his work for many
years in the Irish Writers Centre, Sunflower Sessions and
other venues, including Lime Square Poets on the internet. His
poetry has appeared in *The Baltimore Review, Poetry Ireland
Review, Stepaway Magazine, Flare 7 & 10,* and *Poetry for
a New Ulster, The Wexford Bohemian, The Ken Saro-Wiwa
inspired Collection, Voices from the Land* among others. He has
had a collection of his poetry Although it is Night published
by Wordonthestreet and Lettertec. He has also published two
novels, *Batter the Heart* and *Death in Garrdangan.*

CONTENTS

PART I

Arden, Tullamore, Offaly

Each field could tell its own story
had we but the ear to give it understanding
or time to stand on each overgrown headland,
observing each season since centuries began.

Picture this then, and come to a conclusion:
A field you passed by many years ago, noticed
and then noticed again years later. Now ask:
Does it remember you, and the you in succession?

Even fields that have turned into housing estates --
ones you stood in as a child before now
watching a tractor with plough pulled behind it --
breathes a story the houses can't know.

A Boy on Austin Friars Street, Mullingar

David! David! a boy shouts,
His older sister, embarrassed,
Shoves him on to avoid a pram.

But he is insistent. David! David!
He waves at a young man in
A souped-up BMW, metallic blue.

The boy smiles a beam of sunlight,
He has been recognised with a wink
And a suave nod of the head.

The boy has been recognised,
The Self, made alive to itself,
By a young man, in metallic blue.

A Bus Ride, North Strand, Dublin

It was an evening of grey sky
with the sun scything through
the bland thickness of cloud –
the overhang of jealous autumn
preventing summer from returning.

Nothing exceptional, about this bus
ride, except that instead of riding
upstairs I sat downstairs, traffic side,
by the window, where a shopper from
Clerys and Arnotts demanded gangway

as she plonked herself beside me.
I regretted my choice of seating,
wishing for the cigarette and evening-
paper men upstairs. But I dared not ask
her to move, shift all her baggage,

risk the evil glare -- fear had me
a prisoner. Then, we were halfway
up North Strand, a laneway I had
never noticed before between
a hardware shop and an Italian

fish & chip, a narrow laneway
which seemed to rise toward a
cottage, two windows either side
of an opened half-door and an
elderly woman waited, smiling with

unabashed delight at a girl walking
toward her. A girl, my age, fourteen,
maybe younger, her face
shadowed by evening-burnished hair;
the sun still sheening upon her.

A Café in Harbour Place, Mullingar
Rembrandt's 'Christ on the Cross' 1631

Howard Jones' *'No one is to blame'*
pipes through a café in Mullingar
in the beat and thrust of electronified
syncopation. Am I the only one here
stopping for coffee and a blueberry muffin,

reflecting on Rembrandt's painting
of a sun-deprived, grey-jaundiced
Jesus nailed to a pitch-singed cross
of cheap carpentered wood? Where within
the frame of shrouded silence he realises

his own abandonment, his fear-paralysed
eyes and gnarled screaming mouth tasting
the anguish of hope lost; this same cry
unheard in the agonised etching in an earlier
self-portrait wherein we too become

the Dutchman who has surely painted
the symbol of man as artist forsaken
between speech and dumbness, between
a God absent and the brittle belief in a
rolled-back stone and an empty tomb.

His Christ hangs bereft at our casual forgetfulness,
our walled-out emptiness now brimmed
with desires unfulfilled, and spent treasure
wasting. Is he with us now watching out

for Summer Sales and supermarket trolleys,
this café filling with shoppers and wandered-souls,
heedless of piped music in relentless loop?

Aodhan of Clonard, Co. Meath

Of a winter's dawning the town land he entered;
a stranger who had both the writing craft

and knowledge of bees that was uncommon;
one Patron's day he took himself a local woman,

and for thirty years he lived among us,
sold at the fair, raised two sons, attended the Mass.

Was it true that he once slept by Finian's transept,
worn the habit, and then, one day, just left,

walked through Ballyboggan and never returned?
There is no gravestone in Kinnegad or Clonard

to commemorate the life of this particular man
whose name may have been Aodhan.

A Picture of Heaven
Donnycarney, Dublin

Upstairs on a double decker as we
were going to school, he pulled out
from his battered school bag a magazine,
"Here's a photograph of heaven," he said.

It was of golden brick and stone, blue skies
without clouds, and a lake beside it;
many steps led up to many levels where birds
flew round what seemed a square mansion on top.

"That's where God lives," he declared. We
huddled and oohed, and I tried to count
all the people who managed to get in, and wondered
would my grandparents (they were real old)

get in, and would there be enough room
for them, and by the time I got there
the whole place might not be big enough...
"That's not heaven," a boy from sixth class

sneered, "That's a ziggurat in Babylon."
Disappointment gut me. Where was Babylon?
And what was a ziggurat? At least this
heaven seemed real - as real anyway as

a Dublin city double decker
letting us off at Donnycarney.

A Summer in Cill Ciaráin, Galway.

I

It rained so much one July I read
War & Peace without hardly leaving
the house. Our *Bean an Tí* railed against
the Irish government in Chicago-
gaeilge, served exotic meatloaf dishes
as her daughter dusted and brushed around me
-while Natasha flirted, and Pierre frowned.

II

She'd never been east of the Shannon,
gave birth to seven by the Chicago river;
returned each summer to young *gaelgoiri*
from Tullamore and Terenure, while himself
farmed by the *Trá Mhór* with the dog nipping
strayed cows into the wind-battered shed,
-as weed laden tides eased onto the strand.

III

On *céili* nights we'd sit on a tumbled
down wall as the *cailíni* passed giggling
as gaeilge and smelling of crescent-moon-
petalled stars; but we were too old for them,
they had more interest in downy-lipped boys
they could play with, claim and then discard;
-Natasha, there's a lot yet to be learned.

III

Himself had little English, had been to
Clifden only the once; we conversed with
my smattering of Irish. He'd be *an*
uaigneach, he said when herself was away
with the children in those South Side winters;
he'd be looking towards Boston and beyond,
-as fulmars swept by and woefully keened.

Avila House, Ranelagh, Dublin

I

Stairway
He was trimming the hedge this morning
with clippers, guided by a practiced eye and hand;
I noticed no weeds grew on the gravel path,
and the lawn is daisy-sprinkled, yet trim-green.

His partner, more browned and weather-lined,
though younger, pushes a wheel-rusted
bockety barrow, from bed to bed,
hoeing and raking the clay to an ovular mound.

They stop to smoke a cigarette together facing
the sand-red house, its high grey-slate roof and arrow
head shaped windows; one leaning on the hoe,
the other elbow-crossed sucking into the butt.

I eavesdrop into a moment of their conversation:
"... see that kitchen?" A nod. *"Aye..."*
*"That stairway from there I'd say cuts through to
the centre of the house..."* A silence lingers to absorb

the mystery of the stairway, spiralling up through
the building, its rooms, annexes and alcoves. Yet they
do not desire to walk through the rooms above the kitchen,
just hoe from the rose bed, stand and savour.

II

Garden Agony
A narrow gravel clay-packed path meanders
serpentinely through a row of gnarled
plum trees, arthritically knobbed, black-skinned
as tindered coals, not yet blossomed.

There, beside a clutch of nettles, He could have knelt
drinking His torment. *"It is intolerable that
His disciples slept,"* you said, *"His heart crushed
by the weight of his decision."*

"And what if they were women?" I countered.
They would administer tea, a change of shirt,
given Him consoling embraces like any
mother or lover. There was a consolation

He received not even any woman can give.
Through the twisted path, they led Him,
and on through a gap where once a gate stood,
now rusted and discarded.

III
A Room & A View
Shechem, a well, and a road in Samaria meet,
an inherited field, a water jar and a thirst.
There are no plots of earth so grand and green
as here; this window framing rain-message skies,

chimneys sentineled in a row, the well-placed bush,
and there, a seat. Here, at this car-hum moment
of evening, are rehearsed my clay deceptions;
here, a walled well burrows into my darkness

before a moment's clarity; here, the terror
of the spoken Word awakens the shaded
discriminations of feelings I have held untouched
and untouchable, limned in this evening's solitude;

amidst an aptly placed tree, a seat,
and one black thumbed book.

Awakenings

I

She took my scout's hat, looking for a chase;
I pursued with giggling, feigned annoyance
Around the monastery guest-house until

A monk called a halt to our capering.
It was '68, 'The Long Hot Summer',
Kennedy, King, terms like: 'racial violence',

'Civil rights', differences between 'Black' and
White', 'North' and 'South', were new to me. It was
Before Burntollet: 'Papist' and 'Loyalist'.

Perhaps there is still some old innocence
in me has yet to learn that opposites
Can't be celebrated like 'boy' and 'girl'.

II

The stars and/or whatever did conspire
In the College restaurant, an awkward
Gawky youth to be spellbound by beauty

And fragility. Little did I guess
The strength in your grace; your gift to me:
You allowed me to (say it) love you; a first

Intimacy of the heart - a talisman
From which to bless. In the Municipal
We stood once, gazing at a Leech painting:

A woman, on a parasol afternoon,
Summer green and lilac; you caught me
Attending you, and knew you were beloved.

Boland's Lock, Tullamore.

Was it my great-great-grandfather
or my great-great-great-grandfather
worked on the canal, a carpenter
maybe, who hewed these lock
gates into dams and water
clear ways? An *O'Reilly* from
Cavan is the family lore, started
in Dublin on the Grand Canal,
laboured from lock to lock until

a slip of a girl caught his eye
and he decided to farm her
father's land in Rahan? Was it
here he finally saw the summer
swallow slip and weave among
the rushes, and minded the sun
sinking into the brackened bog
and said, 'it's time to set roots into
land, for these waters will always

be un-rooting, though stilly and slow,
and will remain young always;
but my body needs earth to rest,
and clay to plough, and turf
for to heat my bones'. And so
we have become, and lore and
memory distils generation and
generation to feel the moment
when our journeys dawned.

Buskers & Shop Street, Galway

The Corrib plentifies and flows by Claddagh
Pier, a slow heave toward a soggy green stretch
To Salthill under a not yet blue summer sketch

Of sky. By the Spanish wall, in Capuchin brown,
Where once Columbus may have calculated,
He leans, tenement dreadlocks dangling,

Picking on some kind of Galician hurdy-gurdy;
And chambering through the open Café doorways
A Philippina bows her out-sized fiddle, drawing

Towards a dance-rinse of 'The Bucks of Oranmore'
Complete with her lilting Mindanao swerve;
Down Shop Street a laughing man in a Pink Panther

Suit sklimbers and trinkles an ivory laced xylophone,
Rendering a bounce of Brandenburg Concerto, spiced
With Mississippi blues. Just now, in a swirl of flitting

Shadows, a lemony parrot catches the eye, its lipstick-red
Beak snuggled into its owner's blue canvas hoodie, as they
Slow cycle-weave through somnolent mid-morning shoppers;

And how the Corrib, in a rush of bog-stained water,
Froths a snow remembered glistening of winter;

And how this stolid western town can surprise
Itself with the gift of the unexpected; and yet, too,

'The Foggy Dew' still echoes through a staccato
Laneway, his eyes closing, drunkenly glazed.

Café Ode, Henry St., Dublin

He enters wrapped in a yellow
Sleeping bag, crumpled dirt-black
Hat and asks for some hot water,
His street-stained hands indicating

A small shot measure; he has an
Intelligent but un-scoured face,
A man whose eyes have seen, and ears
Heard, and has come to his own worn

Conclusions. I write this, what, poem,
Reflection, meditation, flash
Fact? I could draw a picture with
Pencil or charcoal had I the

Ability, though I have the
Will, but what does such an act of
Art do, or achieve? I could give
Him a few coins, even some high

Denominations in paper.
I could go out and talk, listen,
Nod, offer some useless advice;
The connection would do us good,

I might feel, but would it? Too late,
He has pulled paper serviettes
From the dispenser, taken some
Sachets of sugar, a couple

Of stirring sticks and has managed,
Somehow, to carry out a full
Plastic cup of cold water as
Well. What can a poem do? What

Has been achieved? Has this been a
Waste, worthless? Nothing has changed as
Far as the street passersby are
concerned. I sit and write, he walks

The street, his yellow sleeping bag
Will cover him at some hostel,
Or doorway; we will pass by with
A sneer, maybe a prayer, but for

The Grace go I, or, I could
'Glut sorrow on a morning rose'.

Canal Walk – Winter, Tullamore, Offaly

Once again, I walk by Srah Castle, its gable-length
cracks still unsettling; yet so it has been down
generational memory, the fissures permanent,
its anonymous history continues. Over the iron
railway bridge the silver-green commuter train
ambles in modern rumbling tones towards Athlone,
thickening the canal path's winter stillness.

I lean over Charleville Bridge and remember
the summer heron stately gliding to its grassy nest,
and swallows darting and swooping over
self-contained moorhens. And, unexpectedly,
my eyes glimpse snowdrops by the water's edge;
blooms of winter encased in a cot of sleep, held
within the delicate momentum of on-sapping-spring.

They may emerge into uncertainty, or, like all
this before me, remain as memorials, encotted
within planetary earth's ever whirling dirge
to death and spring and death and the silent
sonata of the uncertain universe, ever
convulsed in her charted movement
onwards and towards and onwards.

Cathedral Bells, Mullingar, Westmeath

I

On the quarter hour they peal an ancient
Pulse of power through this midland town.
How once we measured fair and market days
As well as rosaries and our daily Mass.

But now, irrelevant and forgotten,
A mere quaint reminder of the hour when
Chasuble and incense floated into
Our particular imaginations -

Here comforting, there terrorizing,
A ritual blessed with grace and a truth,
A ritual ossified to scruples etched,
A conscience formed and a conscience denied.

II

But what quarter bell now sounds its peal and
Pulse to become embedded in the air,
yet again condemned and discredited?

What diligences do we invest lest
Self-forgetfulness and absorption maim
The rage and scream against the new torment?

Why allow those powers yet again deny:
that the tree has a leaf to a branch it
must trust that to the root it is tied.

Christmas in Grandma's, Tullamore, Co. Offaly

On the days before Christmas Grandma made her
greasy mutton stew or her pot of boiled potatoes
swimming in cabbage soup; but for 'afters'

there were mince pies and coffee made the way
the Americans did on TV, the pot percolating
on the Aga, blurting in rhythm into the thick

bottle glass cap; and just behind it proudly
stationed in her special Nenagh Aluminium
pot her pudding boiled with a rattle and pop

to the kitchen radio's *'Jingle Bells'*, or Harry
Belafonte's *'Mary's Boy Child'*, while Grandad
carried in crates of Egan's red lemonade,

and teasing us beyond measure with a feast
of Oatfield sweets and Cadbury's selection boxes.
The rosary of fairy lights strung from building

to building seemed powered by the electric
excitement of children and townsfolk in preparation
for caroling, late wrapping and visits to the Crib.

Even when I was too old for Santa Claus,
as we walked back after Midnight Mass,
I would still imagine him out on his sleigh

skimming across a carpet of stars, delivering
before the Christmas morning light shied him away,
regretting my unbelief as each year passed.

Church of the Assumption, Dalkey, Dublin

They whisper to one another still
on the altar of his sacrifice;

the Last Supper carved in marble,
that neglected discourse of grape and grain.

'Stars are embroidered flowers
on the black cloth that is the night sky';

Basil could speak of such intimacies
as coloured thread, not merely

as metaphor to sweeten the mind,
but projections of the reality

of that which is basic and domestic.
This hushed space, this theatre for the soul,

carved and built in stone and wood,
and the sweat of tradesmen, has forgotten

their laughter, the exhausted step as they
made their way back to their women,

their children; or, their curses trailing loss
outside the local bookie office.

Church Island, Lough Owel, Co. Westmeath

As the ice receded leaving fresh water
to fill the fissures of earth, it was maybe
in the time of the Fir Bolg or the Tuatha
De Danann, they came upon the lake
and felt the island as that sacred place
to which their god had led them.

And their priest and chief stood by its shore
and watched as the sun set in its silent-lit
prayer to the goddess that dwelt there,
she who had waited for them
as bride to their wandering god.

And, on a lunar appointed moment,
the priest crossed and carried with him
the lit torch of an oak branch and planted it
into the menstrual soil and out of it
were born the oracles and laws of the tribe,
and her fresh waters bore trout and fed the land,
fructifying its people. And there then came

a time when belief in local gods
was ridiculed and they recluded
to pre-Cambrian silence, but they hover
still above the lake and the stilled
sleeping goddess awaits those who know
that lake gods are of the one God
that hovered above the waters
where Genesis begins.

Cionn Atha Gad, Co. Westmeath

Names sometimes mean something;
something carried, something borne
upon water, upon the harvesting air
of chaff and seed and hope. The Head
of the Ford of Gad was a place that

would bear fruit, nourish, become
source, locality, field and home. But
'Kinnegad' is an un-tackled plough rusting
on the headland, with farmer and horse
left wandering in the fallowed field.

Croagh Patrick, Co. Mayo

The shifting shale path rooted
to plumb echoless granite;

the grit and lichen path
climbs to a clearing;

the wind-steered shadow
crosses bog and Clew Bay water.

Croghan Hill, Co. Offaly

Here she looms, by the Western road,
sentinel and herald, where our tribal
priests once processed to this umbilicus,

become primordial catechist; their crane
skin bags rattling with chants and runes;
and here I stand with them in contemplation

overlooking these wetland plains; the solstice
sun antiphonates among wasps and bees
swarming around ragwort and nettles,

while to the East cobalt-grey Mount Leinster
withdraws, strumming a sacred paean behind
the slow heave of blackening clouds, and

to the South I watch over the Slieve Bloom
as the Druids might, a sleeping goddess,
her flank clothed in silks of russet and green,

until the shivered mists of night descend,
and she haunts our dreams and awakens
the uncanny as our unassailable companion.

Daddy & Daughter Cycling,
Thomastown, Westmeath

There are no cars parked outside Nanny Quinn's,
the barges lie silent in the cooling summer,
as Royal Canal water, seeped in the clays of peat

and prickly gorse, glides iridescent in cloud-
tufted sunshine. Our lone heron stately sentinels
among companionable moorhen and the swift

swerve of blue gloss-tinted swallows.
The Waterway's towpath has been re-laid,
and where once horses dragged barges through

Abbeyshrule and returned commercially laden
to the Dublin docks, now in the new logistics
and imposed contingencies of lockdown

and social distancing, I take my routine canal walk.
Old dusted down Raleigh bikes and children
wearing safety helmets gather; a father cycles by

in shorts and summer shirt, his daughter on the
carrier seat, familiar now to his tack and turn, sitting
in the safe swerve and glide of her pre-bridal dance.

Donegal Remembered

On a bus tour through the Julian Alps,
vertigo-towering, mica-pocked, we swing
and twist our way by the Triglav, through cart-
narrow roads and pass a single stone cottage

tied precariously to an escarpment.
It is surely like Donegal in its
isolation. When the winter snows come
tumbling in how can that woman make it

to a shop some twenty miles away, down
careening ledges of rock-infested
valley? She will be snow-bound, literally
hibernating; as house bound as that

Donegal widow I once mused would be
on a rain-lashed Sunday morning as she
might pray her holy picture-stuffed missal
instead of making it to Sunday Mass.

Dublin on a May Evening

After I randomly attended Friday Evening Prayer
in the Pro-Cathedral, I sit inside Burger King
on O'Connell Street watching a Buddhist monk
wearing a canvas fishing hat, and a tan linen jacket,
as he begs, extending a bronze dish,
his benign smile accepting the unexpected.

Father and son, draped in Bohemian football scarves,
saunter towards Dalymount for a rendezvous
at a pub on Doyle's Corner, while a Nubian Princess
passes by the window looking for the 16A, but walks on,
maybe considering the Luas as a better option.

A motorised wheelchair silently glides by as his
walking partner nods in silent agreement, carrying
a Supervalu shopping bag. A Spanish girl, cinder
hair with stringy blue streaks, her iPhone tight
to her ear, gesticulates impatience, and with suppressed
panic, flicks a reefer tilted delicately in her left hand.

Maybe if I were a fisherman, I would now
be imbibing the prairie plains of a greying ocean,
my mind reaching beyond any visible horizon,
or maybe a farmer, standing in this evening silence
contemplating the swallow-dash-sweep over
hope-bearing meadows, pondering the harvest,
sniffing the air, deciphering cloud formations.

But time costs money when you park your car in Dublin
[over three quid an hour]. How much am I willing to spend
to sit, watch, enjoy this rare splash of a May evening sun
dip behind the skeletal shadow of the Carlton? There go
some stray hen-party girls in tight bulging jeans and shorts,
legs, hands, face, spray-tanned, pink sparkles pasted
to cheek and forehead, giggling an anticipated night
of clubbing, revelry, drunken kisses and forgetfulness.

Our new Irish-Africans, Brazilians and East Europeans
walk by; they have no thought of the Friday evening's
reading from Galatians, nevertheless, a harvest of patience,
kindness and generosity, might be in evidence among them,
and, if not, if muted, at least Paul's twelve virtues reside

in the mansions of these passing-by souls and in the salt sweep
of wave on shingle, and in the tree swish across the headland
boundaries where the random ordinary embraces
the richness of risk-inducing possibilities.

The monk has disappeared, father and son a memory,
the iPhone girl long gone, but a ringlet-haired child in
Communion frock skips by, carefree, holding her mother's
hand, her pearl purse and white dress-shoes flounce and dance.

And now the Nubian Princess returns, a revenant of Africa,
bathed in the same sun as it dips where her mind and soul
might be, her moments and places, her waiting here.

Encounter with a Buddhist Monk
Drumcondra, Dublin

The suburban garden blushed primrose
and hollyhocks at the pre-Cohen concert
party; blue-tit nipped at grub and flitted

fearfully with sudden laughter and squeal
of welcome with offers of tea, Chablis,
or whatever you're having yourself.

"We lived in the same neighbourhood
in Montreal, I was pretty much washed
out on drugs, drinking pretty heavily.

I happened to walk into a café
that he liked. I had just bought his first
album. We sat beside each other, had

some kind of conversation. I can't
remember much about it, I was pretty
much out of it. He was too." Sean smiled

under a baseball cap, pain and wasted
memories turned sardonic and forgiven.
He wore an orange sweater and sensible

brogues. I thought of a long-suffering wife,
a wild daughter rebelling and sullen.
"I'm a Buddhist monk, now, living on

a mountain in Spain." Are these the kind
of conversations one might encounter
with certain kinds of men? In Waterford,

for instance, two centuries ago: Edmund:
"I had that sea chandler's business on the quays,
sold it and now teach poor boys in that old

stable I bought off Barrack Street." Or,
Antony presenting that moment
of surprise and uncomprehending

puzzlement: "I walked into the desert
and kept walking until I could hear
daimon silences singing in the sand."

Famine Walk, Strokestown – Dublin.
A Child's Bronze Shoes,
Thomastown, Co. Westmeath.

I

Commemorate by canal water where
spring morning shimmers funereal
in the sun's warmth; when a week ago
the bailiff came with black-helmeted

Constabulary and an eight foot rough-hewn
battering ram thudded and crunched
while inside the unlit cabin his sister

has enfolded him in her child-maternal
arms, their father anger-spent, defeated,
kneels beaten on the mud floor, and mother
coughs tubercular blood into a fetid rag;

by mid-day the four are huddled in a ditch
dependent on the kindness of strangers, but
numbed to the rebuffs of heartless winds.

II

Commemorate by sea water where
spring-tide pulls the morning refugees
in a rubber dinghy where twenty bodies lie;
his sister enfolds him in her child-maternal

arms, unknown men lie against them huddled
and defeated, their dying mother slips silently
into the black maw of the funereal Channel.
And what awaits if they are beached on a wind-

rebuffed strand, the kindness of strangers,
or care-less disdain? These child's bronze shoes
scream to us of a history of Landlord and Warlords
enriched by the ridding of such inconveniences.

Fisherman on the Garavogue, Sligo

He stands, blue baseball cap and chest waders,
knee high in dun green water; with flick
of a wrist he pays out the line, drawing
it in, flicking again in rhythmic swoops
of green loop, arcing in a slow motion

dance with the late evening sun. Two swans
and their five fluff-grey cygnets glide towards
the weir, turn and return, at home in their
domain, eyeing both fisher and trout as
they break surface rising to the sedge.

Do you catch many? I ask. He turns with a wink,
*'Sure, isn't that the game of it. If you don't
cast you don't catch'.* And do you keep
them all? *'I return them to the river;
but keep a salmon - if I manage to catch one'.*

Fleadh Cheoil Harp Competition, Mullingar

And up he stepped carrying his harp
hefted at the pillar, and you'd say,
or, could have said, I seen that young

lad playing for the Shamrocks at
half-back or half-forward, against
the Ballycastle Gaels, good on his feet,

up for the high ball. And you'd think,
Naw, it couldn't be. But there he is
taking the community hall chair,

setting up his harp, his athletic
fingers strumming, testing its tone
and its coloratura, and whether the

sweetness of sound would float, hold
in the hall and pounce at the ear and heart;
pounce like he would for a loose ball

and sail it, with a sweet left foot, over
the black spot. And you'd think, who is
this young lad, one of our under-fifteens?

Where did the seraph come from
all of a sudden, how did he arrive
here at the Fleadh harp competition?

And you'd be struck by the re-echo of,
Why should we be surprised? Why
expect him to be other than the sensitive

soul borne upon myth and song and be
arrived here, his Keds tapping and
his fashionably knee-ripped jeans?

Franciscan Abbey, Multyfarnham, Westmeath
Founded 1270

Stone upon individual hand-masoned stone,
feet and knee-smoothened, buckled grey
and black, each locked into the other, until

this space encloses to silence. Footsteps
outside on crunching gravel, a lawnmower,
the seasonal voices of daily doings, shimmers

within these Abbey walls. This is not a place
of escape, a running away from, but a reclamation
of what is fragile and reed swaying. This space,

beyond the border of madness and serenity,
has become necessary, else we descend into
the dark heart's abyss where stones form, where

they crack and crumble become sterile soil, where
no seed can grow, or, if it falls, they split and wither.

God is in His Heaven...
Sisters of Charity, Howth, Dublin

The convent smelled always of buttery
shortbread and shone of fragrant wax, with
rhythmic clicking of black wooden rosary
beads, and a swish of copious cloth,
heads bowed, eyes guarded in decorum,

as laid down by religious regulation.
I played soccer on their grass tennis court,
kicking the ball into the drooping net.
Our Sunday visit; an old nun sat
in a brown stoned alcove reading from

a black leather-bound prayer book;
my aunt and mother in quiet conversation
about family, children and sickness.
An adventure it was from Artane to Howth,
riding on a green double decker, a chatty

bus conductor and a driver isolated in his
noisy cockpit -- past Dollymount reminding me
to ask: "Can we swim? Can we swim?"
and: "Can we walk to the cove?"
"Can we climb to the lighthouse?'"

Did God live only in places that were
shiny and silent? What happened to Him
when we closed the heavy wooden convent gate
and walked through a blackberry lane
of thistles and wild wind-swayed grass?

Would He have walked the pebbled shingle cove
as we played by an abandoned boathouse
-- we, in a reverie of oil-skinned fishermen
and sea rescues -- He, in the sand crunch of sea,
echoing anger into the cliff above when the sun

was hidden behind thunder grey clouds?
The return of a smiling sea at a sudden sun-burst
brought, "Can we swim? Can we swim?"
It was always too wildly noisy, and unpredictable.
"Let's get back for tea," my aunt would say.

Tea was served with stiff linen serviettes
and shallow china cups -- a formality which
starched any compulsion to get to the chocolate
biscuits first. In convents where God lived,
you waited your turn, were polite and didn't

let your mother down, even in front of aunts
who wanted to indulge. After the evening bell
for prayer, we would leave in a hurry because
God was waiting in the chapel and she must not
keep Him waiting. On board the bus the conductor

with a Sunday evening smile chatted about hurling
and asked me, who I wanted to win, Kilkenny or
Tipperary? I wanted Tipp to win (Tom and Noel's
father was from Nenagh, and I did not want
to disappoint), even though I was a Leinster man,

and felt the tug of loyalty to my native province.
I wondered which team God would want to win --
but He would not even be at Croke Park.
He was in a convent by the sea,
waiting patiently for my aunt.

Harbour Street, Tullamore, Co. Offaly

Here are Sunday afternoon shoppers where another
time ago the silence of religious observation
hung penitentially, or, on occasion, a club

match in O'Connor Park might see a procession of men,
cigarettes in hand, nervously anticipating
county glory. I smell petrol fumes now, but also there,

in the air, unexpectedly, the smell of animal
piss, that clean sharp tang must have seeped into
these stones and cement grooved paths, released

now to stagger memory into life: calves slipping
and slithering down green urine slopped trailers;
pigs, pink and manure slathered, squealing in riotous

protest as farmers, nicotine fingered, Wellingtons
stuffed with brown stained dungarees, turn
and twist them into display. Smell has tricked me

into hearing my Grandmother, sending me to
Wrafters for a pound and a half of back rashers,
"And make sure he gives you Tullamore sausages".

He still stands there behind the counter, flour dust
in his hair, slicing bacon; the smell of stale Guinness
lingering from behind the yellow glass frosted door.

"You too will be a memory like me, young fella."
He wraps the sausages in grease paper, "Others will
remember you for the ordinary oul' things."

Hermitage Diarmuid
Castledermot, Co. Kildare

I will build by water
a hut of mud and thatch

carve four crosses on
the four corners of a field

enclose my soul in
darkness where only

a candle will be lit
and on a lintel of stone

kneel.

In the Townland of Ardrum, Roscommon.

There it has crouched, limp, lost and alone,
between Athlone and Lecarrow, in the townland
of Ardrum, in a meadow field, seven paces
from the road, a Charles Burrell & Sons' steam

traction engine abandoned through decades of journeys
West as a child and adolescent, to these adult
years. Once, this powered farming machinery with
the flap and thud of a continuous leather belt.

And what was liveried in enamel-hardened
Lincoln Green and Royal Blue turned rust-mould,
is now a rain-and-wind-scoured random
installation, sun-buffed and frost-annealed

to a smooth sand-iron surface. And what now
might its unintended function be as it resides
in this summer scented field? A memory catcher,
fermenting continuous fly-wheel moments?

Inis Muireadach
Monastic Site Co. Sligo

Ferried across by a fishing boat
stinking of diesel and the stolid

stomach churn smell of fish,
we swayed with breast-soft heave

of sea to Saint Muireadach's
wind-rebuffed island.

By goat-path and gull-height where
granite uterus-black purgatories

begat, in cruel ecstasy, the
annihilation of God-violated

bone, dare I linger and test a
hunger for sea-salt bite and

desolation's searing cleansing?
A cormorant in flight, belly

crossed to the waves, carries my
cowardly heart, shambling shorewards.

Journeys North

I

Tunnelling through the darkness, our train
is rail-cornering into south Armagh.

Memory conjures the roll of hill, green
ditch, the breeze-swirl of squared meadows.

That resolute boy defended the Ulster
Gap here with spear-shaft and javelin-justice.

The Bull was safe. He slaughtered his nine
hundred by the banks of the bravely exposed bog

where the stink of kin-blood seeps into
the fold and frounce of the black Cooley.

Have we come to Belfast already,
to Victoria's iron and glass? We gather

our cases and stuff newspapers into bags,
while outside blobs of rain slap and bullet

against the window's mirrored blackness.
I frown at my forgetfulness:

I have no coat with which to brave the elements.

II

As long as I listen to this cassette, recorded
from an old LP, Don McLean will forever
sing with sweet nostalgic lilt, up to:
"But for all his great powers, he's wishful like me..."

The rest is mangled by the mindless vindictiveness
of a record needle skipping and leaping through
scratch-slashed hairline vinyl grooves.
At that moment his voice sucks into

the black hole of permanent dumb oblivion,
until he returns again, *"... to the sea."*
Though the intervening words have disappeared,

Memory and Rote preserve what enervated engineering
has so wantonly destroyed, but is still sung and ached for:
"To be back where the dark Mourne sweeps down..."

III

As you drove North within sight of that radio mast,
like an aerated rusted skyscraper, it always happened:
Gay Byrne's Morning Show, *"... a listener in Glasnevin*
has a question about her chrysanthemums..." would
crickle-crackle and disappear into the ethered space

of prickly static as plummy Auntie Beeb
tracked through with warnings of *'... heavy traffic*
south of Mannings Heath...' and '... the M60
out of Manchester going west is clearing,
police advise caution due to flooding...'

IV

The Sperrins, lie like a family spaniel,
acknowledging stranger and friend;
not minding how I journeyed, the only Southern
registered car between Dungannon and here,

driving through the open-air shopping
thoroughfare of Cookstown, and welcomed
into Londonderry in uncertain decal alphabet,

with Union Jacks frayed yet flapping, Orange
and Gospel Hall claiming history in the places
where your family of farmers and teachers
gave you root and your 'feel for books', where you

played football for Castledawson, walked the roads
and wind-shook fields of Mossbawn, Broagh, Anahorish,
and returned here completing your 'ring of affection'.

Killybegs, Co. Donegal: St Mary's Parish Church

I
It weighs on me these memories of her;
what was, is gone, what might have been, unknown
and unknowable. One brief moment
of encounter fires and explodes and ripples
and ripples and still the heart aches and is storm-
tossed; out of the depths of a forgetfulness
where there is no forgetting – a memory

alive now and quaking. She sat and prayed
here, maybe thought of me and added
a special blessing for my wellbeing. Does she
think of me now? Does she wonder what became
of me? With iridescent callousness
you have placed in our hearts so much capacity
to feel, to love, but also loss and its pain.

II
Above the tabernacle in stained glass grey and white,
St. Catherine leans on the altar of crucifixion,
exhausted, waiting with stigmata and crown
of thorns, pleading, hoping. But you, past pain, you knew
it too: God-abandonment, hanging there the promise

scourged and cleansed of any and all deceit, Christ
of the sea and the black depths of memory never
to be relived or relieved, tangled into that thorny
crown clutching at the scutch of hope, the heart
as yet unhealed and maybe unhealable.

Lake Derravaragh, Co. Westmeath

The swans of Lir have departed but their three
hundred year keening is not just a myth stored
in our tribal memory. Their exile and fragile hope
have become this lakeside birdsong. The low
grey sky resonates with their oratorio of loss.

The mallard and teal continue to ruffle-scavenge
within the green plush of these secretive
bulrushes where fishermen row through water
path-ways and plash out into this storied lake

to cast their line and await the nip and nab
of the same pike and trout the four
white-swanned children once pleaded to be
the companions of their desolate waiting.

Lough Owel, Co. Westmeath, New Year's Eve

Facing the fading sun,

a rain-heavy stretch of ebony cloud
veils the lake like a theatre curtain
hiding the anticipated scenes behind.

And then unprepared and unexpected
the pale sun sudden burst burnishes yellow-gold
in the full gleam of the West's momentary announcement:

All is symbol of the un-comprehendible,
rendered real upon Owel's slate still winter water,
its andante-descending afterglow.

Meelick Church, Friarsland, Galway
Built by Papal Permission 1415
Erected 1474

A moorhen glides where history has not scoured;
by Norman stone on native soil the host
is elevated still.
                        By silent Shannon water
the January sun sleeps where I,
a pilgrim, strayed upon unremembered
footprints the moorhen has disdained.

Megalithic Site
Loughcrew, Oldcastle, Co. Meath

Here he must have stood...

- had he been
tending to a lamb?
by this ditch standing?
just strolling by?
or journeying?
maybe in silence,
waiting? -

... and looked there where the sun
danced through a meadow of grass,
and noted where the sky
and the earth's black sod
became one,

become
another place.

Did he say:
Here
could all our fears,
our hopes, desires,

our hates, our pain
and loves be held?

Or
did he just feel it so?

Did he sense
that where all desire
and hope and pain were held

then the better be contained
for the moment of death to anneal --

and the place of birth be made?

Motte, Granard, Co. Longford

In this country you can't go far without coming
upon a place, like here, where you can stand
on an evening with clouds speckling the blue
blanket above, and below discover a pre-historic
landscape, where you can cast an eye over five
counties, view a town, the grey silvered edges
of a lake, a scattering of farms, a statue of Patrick

planted in defiance and triumph, now a cow-path
for tourists, and note the Convent of Mercy
abandoned, its veiled and pious women forgotten,
and hear a group of teenage girls giggling at some
gossip, unaware their grandmothers feared and were
awed by them once; a Midland town shadowed

by a Motte rooted to a seam of brittle limestone,
preserved by a brown truss of marinating bog.

Old Croghan Man, Co. Offaly.

Found 2003

There must be chosen from the tribe
A 'bridegroom of the goddess', sacrificed

In the sacrum space of their ritual-shaping
Mind, born of the fear of her withholding;

Unless he dies and the blood seed of his
Virility soaks the uterine nidus of her body,

Unsatisfied lust and greed will brew their
Bog-barren fields to a non-incubating death.

On the Eighth Day - Mountain
Howth, Co. Dublin.

I

On the eighth day, before the dawn chirped to our awakening,
we came down to the kitchen and buttered sandwiches
beneath a solemn light; the muffled clatter of delph and knives
clicking on breadboards, rippled through a self-imposed silence.
With RSV underarm, I walked to the Hill of Howth.
Pleasure boats sat eschew on the inlet mud-flats,
and the seafront wall had no tide to make welcome.

The waking sun etched myriad sparkles on glass-grey water,
trailing inexorable ripples into a sleep quiet city.
On Bull Island a stooped figure probed the sand for fish bait;
and the sun burnt the morning's mist to a clarity, unveiling deep
pastel-blue mountains behind Dun Laoghaire.
A gull lay dead in feather-flutter, entangled in a ditch,
Announcing the teetering poise in any seabird's flight.

II

All day you threatened to cut a furtive
track along the twisting pathways of the cliff,
and along the shingle crunching underfoot.
By four o'clock your sudden smoke-sooty
cloud vanquished the sun and blackened the bog
dark sea, and in an instant of searing
clarity, felled me you to prostration;
I hoped no one was watching; the arched cliff
darkened to a monastic cell, a heart-

pulse beat to the thud of wind, riveting
sea to stone, bone to lichen-pocked rock,
flesh to worm bait and a dead seagull.
That evening we returned, and broke the Bread
of solitude at the altar, where candle
flames spurted and hissed into flutters
of stillness; afterwards we cooked
a meal to celebrate an ageless pattern
poised within the daemon of chaos.

Parliament Street, Dublin
Traces Left Behind

Crossing at the traffic lights on
Parliament Street, and making his
Way over Capel Street bridge he
Processed in priest-like dignity
Bearing, in one hand, an opened
Tin of John West sardines, and in
The other, a white plastic fork.

He vestured a power-blue business
Suit-jacket, a faded open-
Necked white buttoned shirt, and trousers
Paper-stiff with grime; he had the
Gaunt middle-aged demeanour of
A solicitor. No one took
Heed of him, no one smiled, or turned
To snigger at his sockless feet

as he padded the asphalt,
the rubber soles of his Adidas
shoes dragging like
perverse flippers
behind him.

Pastoral, Ard, Geashill, Co. Offaly

"It was a thoroughly poor June. The worst in forty years..."
The grey tractor thundered around the three acre
green-heavy end field, felling at their ankles
brigades of grass, laying it out in neat rows

ready for the turning and the steel whipped churning
of the baler. "This time last year we had it saved
within in the shed... I drained this field myself...
Remember how it was three years ago?

Sunk it with a plough and spade, and drove
a trench abroad to the ditch... Best bit of a field
ever you saw in a long time..."
Before we bought the tractor, the horse came

out of retirement for three days' sweat and pungent
leather. We forked hay into head high domes,
scattered across the clay burnt stubble before a nightfall
rain drizzled. Then, when the sun promised heavy heat,

and before clouds gathered again, we carted them into
the shed. All day we sweated and scratched
from the heat and the dust, slowly composing
a rick that would stand us the winter. "Build

from the outside in and keep the centre filled..."
At night, too tired to watch TV we sat together
in the unlit kitchen, drinking tea, gazing out
at the balloon-red sun slipping down the window,

beyond Cleary's long field, beyond the purple
Slieve Bloom, of the clean and soft cut.

Prams on a Village Green, Dunboyne, Co. Meath.

'My friends think I'm crazy', she said through
tightly stifled tears. 'But I see mothers and babies
sitting on the park bench and wheeling their prams,

and I talk to them, they're so real; but when I turn around
they disappear. I'm scared there's something wrong with me'.
This village was where a Mother and Baby Home

was once located. I assure her I do not believe
she is going crazy. These mothers have returned to
reveal what suffering they went through and what

the village refused to see. 'But when will I stop
seeing them?' Her hands scrunched into fists.
'When we no longer need to be seen', they replied.

Randomed, Parnell Square, Dublin

A barman's strike brought him to
the National Ballroom. It was a fundraiser.
He did not bring his Current Girlfriend;
but then he caught sight of a young woman,
red hair, laughing eyes, and graceful elegance.

We still are not sure who made the first move;
he claimed she came over to him; she claimed
he asked her out for a dance. Does it matter?
It was random, without method, without
planning, but without doubt it took place.

And somehow, here I am, retelling that event
outside the same address. But there is a coda
to this story. He told us he happened
to be reading the local obituaries, and there,
he said, he discovered what had happened

to that Current Girlfriend; her funeral
had just taken place in the local parish church;
she had died leaving a husband and family behind,
and had lived on the same road as us.
And who, or what, randomed that?

Reading Ulysses in Mullingar Cathedral

Persecution, says Bloom, all the history
of the world is full of it. Perpetuating
national hatred among nations.

What is your nation, if I may ask,
says the citizen. Ireland, says Bloom,
I was born here. The citizen said nothing
only cleared the spit of his gullet.

On Bishopgate Street a child rides
nervously on his new bike, his hijab
covered mother trailing behind. Walking
by the Joe Dolan [life-size] statue a girl
reads from a letter to her mother, hesitating
over each word: '...the appointment must be
confirmed before the date otherwise...'
The mother asks something in Polish,
the girl repeats more confidently.

These mosaics of St Patrick and St Anna
were commissioned by the Bishop of Meath,
designed and executed in the Marian Year
by Boris Anrep, muse of Akhmatova.

A nation, says Bloom, is the same people
living in the same place. By God, then,
says Ned, laughing, if that's so I'm a nation
for I'm living in the same place for the past five
years. Bloom says, trying to muck out of it:
Or also living in different places.

Sea Raven, North Atlantic, Co. Mayo

There is the Sea, the blank, bottomless blackness,
And its klaxon proclamation to the inscrutable waves
Splicing into splinters of ice in the High Atlantic maelstrom,
Heaving Sea Ravens onto the vast tides of demented

Daimonia, roiling them onto the sharp rock edges of the
Landsmen's prow, where they perch, clasp and cling,
To thrive and dive and thrust downwards to their
Limited depths, never to see and create a name for the

Abyssal creatures that survive there. And yet how
We reach out beyond and into imagined celestial beauty,
And further out to the marvel of the stars athwart our ken
To seek escape there in perfect unimaginable fantasy,

While Terror paralyses our dive to Sea Raven depths.

Seeing at D'Arcy's Bridge, Royal Canal, Co. Westmeath

I have been walking this canal trail for months
but had not seen until now these two barges rusted
to cinder-brown, a side-by-side effigy, not abandoned
but buried in a water-grave of lime citrus algae,

a hawthorn as headstone and bull rushes as pall
and wreath. Could it be that the winter
light had just now turned spring-revealing?

These wind-bent reeds must have exposed this
surprising moment of seeing, a canal siding
dug out probably sixty years ago especially for these
twins of obsolescence, and, as with all forgotten

graves that become unnoticed except for the
careless random passerby, guilt upon seeing
what ought to have been memory-reverenced.

Shannon Crossing

Out of Cootehall I crossed where
the princely Shannon sleeps and plugged
my recording mind into the ambient
silence of warblers and intermittent

cock-crow piercing the distance between
the bees reminiscing and the green
metallic-shine of dragonflies
floating on a bog-black meniscus.

II

In the Church of Our Lady
of Clonfert two women enter,
one carrying her dog, and kneel
at the medieval Madonna wood carving

placing their anxieties and daily
frets at her feet, hoping her
embrace will soothe their individual
circumstance of loss and longing.

III

My evening garden is in green
repose, held now within the width
of a nano-second sliver of the universe
as she spins in gigantic gyrations,

and I stand under the surgent moon
and store these memories between
a Shannon crossing and the Madonna
centuries stilled behind glass.

Srah Castle, Tullamore, Co. Offaly

Above the first cut of silage,
a numberless squadron of crows
crowd and swirl in the wind blue sky;

the field, yellow tufted and spare,
the soil retaining the odour of esker sand,
while there on a lush green harbour,

where the harvester could not enter,
it stands, fo'c'sle-grey, broken bridge
and keel unperturbed by the witness

of its own ruin, the raptor crows
wing-tussle, descend and greedily glean.

Summer 1966
Church of the Assumption, Tullamore

We were ten years old kicking
a ball around the church yard.

On the plinth of the statue
of Christ the King he saliva-

fingered a map of the world
and said, "The British Empire

takes in here, here, here and here,"
sweeping a finger and smudging

until his globe was filled,
the white stone darkening

under his handiwork. Later
I asked Grandad, "Is it

true that the English own
the whole world?"
      "Go back

and tell that fella they never
owned us."
      They had just

won the World Cup. "Yiz'll
never win it again," I said.

Stonecrop
The Burren, Co. Clare

Even our assumptions have been brutalised;
there are no certainties, nor a guaranteed
future. We have come to a time and a place
where we cannot imagine Sisyphus happy.

We have built a labyrinthine maze
and discovered we have lost ourselves
within it, become trapped in what we have
created. And yet, we know as knowing

becomes conscious, that an impulse
to annihilation contradicts the core cravings
of our marooned souls. We may see,
and at times weave the pattern of death,

but there breathes within us the denial
of obliteration and the realisation
of the hidden dictations of the heart.
For, we may die; what we have created,

worked for, and have given birth to,
will return to the parched sands of the desert.
Yet, another impulse binds us together
and in turn transcends the limits of our knowing,

which implies our freedom to choose either
the embrace of ultimate annihilation, or the
willingness to accept what cannot be proven nor denied:
the trust of this storm-beaten cliff-side flower.

The Big Drain, Harbour Street, Tullamore, Co. Offaly

The big drain was filled to its brim with
rainbow-greased inky water where
cars my grandad repaired were washed.

The yard flooded during heavy
summer thunder showers and we'd be
shin high in wellingtons while

he would sweep dirt turned sloppy
mud into the drain. After flooding
I would be warned about playing

near the drain, but I never heeded.
Then one day I got a brand new
Matchbox military ambulance,

its tiny red cross stamped on camouflage
green. Peter pleaded with me to let him
play with it. I warned him not to play

near the drain, but he did not heed.
I watched it slip out of his hands
and roll into the watery maw. My panic

turned to angry scream and a nodule
of knowledge thumped in my chest.
It was lost. Forever. It would not be

replaced, they said. After all you
were warned to stay away. But you
could open the drain, get it out, I pleaded.

It's gone, they said. Down into the
netherworld of the town sewage
system. But it was not my fault, I cried,

He did it, probably on purpose,
out of jealousy. I never asked him back
to play, have no memory of ever

seeing him again – only that
first knowledge of a perversity
that is inheld in all things desired.

The Battle of Mainistir, Limerick, 1579

In revenge for Drury's ignominious defeat,
Captain Maltby, with thumbscrew and
iron-hooped headband ravaged by Lough Gur.

The Irish sympathisers of Desmond lay dying
by ditch and callows, their Bishop, O'Healy,
clamped in roasted iron boots, his tongue

cleaved from his throat, gurgling blood,
baying a scream-dumb death. Their fields
scorched, the peasants reeled yet again, as

Fitzmaurice, their hero, was slain at Barrington
Bridge. By Bruff and Croom, Maltby formed
his line, his back to the smooth shallows

of the Maigue; John Desmond's Gallowglass
waited in the woods at Kilmore. The English
camp lay shrouded in the silent river mist while

the clans perched in the trees waited, their
cries rising into a crazed fever by the hour.
The Papal Standard was displayed.

*The Jesuit, Allen, distributed Benediction
and Assurances of Victory:* Rome would
rejoice in the defeat of the heretic English.

Through the indecipherable gutturals of Spain
the officers made known their dispositions
to the wild pagan Irish who shouted a curdling

hubbub in their Ancient Gaelic. Screeching
war pipes raised the thick fog. Maltby's drum
beat his English to quarter. His pikemen bearing

eighteen feet of wooden lance, their steel tips
rattling formed squares with musketry enfiladed.
And still they waited, their backs to the daunting river.

The fearsome noise of Gallowglass, frenzied into
battle-lust, its unruly crescendo undulated across
the dewy fields of Mainistir. The Spanish officers

marked the line, tried to steady the ranks, but
bursting with blood-madness the Gallowglass
charged naked into the English musket and pike,

chopping their way through a forest of shafts
while wave after wave of Gaelic axmen plunged
into the English ranks of musket and steel,

their discipline exhausted by Irish savagery.
And the younger sons of Desmond did fight,
met Maltby face to face, lay slain on the field

of blood. Thomas, the son of John Og, and Edmond,
son of Turlough Mac Sheehy and a great
number of the Constables of the Clann Sheehy,

great spoils of weapons and military attire
left on this occasion to Captain Maltby's people.
The English, triumphant by the blood-muddy

fields of Mainistir, found there under the many
corpses piled, the slain body of the Jesuit,
Allen, sword in hand. He fell *a prophet of Baal.*

And the remnant of Desmond through
the tangled woods of the Maigue escaped;
and Maltby's English in autumn-sheeting rains,

marched in pursuit, ague-tired and stricken,
and for forage found only burnt earth
before them on the road to Askeaton.

The Lily of Easter, GPO, Dublin

Walking down O'Connell Street one matinee
afternoon, I saw her at the GPO standing
behind a makeshift trestle table;

(There are shrapnel dents still in the --
are they Doric or Corinthian? -- columns).
She was selling *An Phoblacht and Long Kesh*

memorabilia and was to me a Maud Gonne become
old and pap-withered. Her grey green pain
drilled eyes still haunt my memory

of her at her table. I sentimentalize
her in a bed-sit off Blessington Street,
making late winter fires on an ash grate

with back issues of her unsold propaganda
and only the remnants of passion,
sputtering into a fatigued innocence.

She will never do battle with sword, fist or gun --
her realities are memories of warrior heroes,
once reckless for sacrifice and careless death.

The Well-field, Knock, Co. Mayo

With a chipped enamel bucket my
Granny would send me up to the well-field.
"We'll have that for the spuds," she'd say.

And I would step down onto the worn
flinty stone, dip and wait the drag
of water to glop fill the bucket and lift.

I marvelled always at the clean sheen
of spilled spring water as I heaved
that bucket out of the silvered silence,

and onto the breeze shimmered grassy ditch.
I would then bowl my hands, scoop
and gulp water so sweet, so cold tangy clean,

my heart heaved with simple delight.
And I received images then of the others
who had come to this magic harnessed place:

those past generations of Mayo farmers,
that pre-historic man who first stood here,
staked his claim, marked this place as holy,

and fathered me, generation down generation.

This Is Never Going To Go Away
North Frederick Street, Dublin

This is never going to go away, you know;
this low sun-blinding street at evening
just before the night chases its crossing
shadow over the city, and westward

ensnares the sloping midland bog. This
will be how the pulse of the painter
will enroot into rust-rustling woods
and be daubed onto the prepared canvas

where stalking shadows will be stirred
into the sweep and flounce of colour. This
then is eternity's first moment of creation,
this low sun-blinding evening street.

Turraun Wetlands, Pullough, Co. Offaly

I
Wetlands and Church
A local clay fired in local kilns
to form a brick, to build this church,
these homesteads, above layer upon layer
of millennial-seeped bog until roots

settle to foundation become compulsion
to avoid the unmooring life of the wanderer,
where now they walk, trade, dance, sing,
birth a family and become tied to this land;

sculpt history out of bog-oak and fire-coloured
glass, satisfying the rarefied impulse; to celebrate,
memorialise, mourn, curse, hold one another,
incarnated to their story, their wetlands;

farm soggy clay into fructed fields;
wait upon the good days for cutting turf,
the cotton sway of breeze, the ashen green
heather, the canvas splash of yellow furze.

II
Church
Tabernacle
Heart shaped bog oak seeped
in aeon-marinated floor,
entombed in the still and silent
gestating blackness,
to flame and thorn sacrificial hearts.

Lectern
Ageless-milled branches reach,
enroot, embrace the trauma
of the Word, seeking, pleading,
perennially unsatisfied.

Baptismal Font
A hand of delicate fingers holds
new life that could migrate
to a fist, a grip, a destroyer-force,

a tender touch, lingering;
a trunk of oak rings demarcating
time, naming its beginning;

a ripple of the universe, a stone
plunged into the still layer
upon layer of eternal time,

stacked one on another
to the final moment of God's hand
holding, embracing,

crushing, destroying, turning
to dust the clay that was bed
for the seed planted and replanted,

decaying and re-decaying
from seed to fallen seed
set into flourishing clay.

Votive Candle Stand
I will light a candle
to commemorate the heart's flame
tortured with thorn and fears
transubstantiated to hate,
anger, and destruction.

I will light a candle
as a flame of hope,
its tongue of fire to sear callous
stupidity, a cathartic burn
to eradicate diseased desire.

I will light a candle
to dispel the darkness of this
encroaching night;
and though I have left this place,
it will be a light still

when grey-blue dawn emerges
into these wetlands of shallow fields,
the sleeping and waking children
who remain here, concierge
to residual thaumaturgy of place.

PART II

Anchorage:
Psychiatric Ward, VA Medical Center, Perry Point, Maryland, USA

I

The Susquehanna is bay-wide at this Point,
and aeon-deep on this November-chilled
Chesapeake water; it is the brown month
when earth's duty it is to strip to a clarity

the scowl of skulking death. A barge, ferrying
quarried stone and pushing a heave of water out
into the grey-blue-banked distance could be
transformed into an idea, a floating acorn,

or a meniscus-held dragonfly, ever a notion
for canvas and frame; but death could never be
an idea, a metaphor to protect delicate sensibilities.
Season's duty by the Susquehanna is the port of call

for exhausted geese, belly-flapping by funeral-leafy
trees onto this water, announcing death; but not of
incense and black cloth, nor of clay piled to the knees
of a solitary mourner, not this death.

II

At this Point, where river becomes bay,
and bay invites the uncertainty of storm
and the shift of a Chesapeake tide, the mind
may anchor, seeking refuge from too many
unrelenting defeats, may drift with water's suppleness
out to sea, become rage-gripped by knowledge,
cold-sumped with the certainty of death's echo

pounding on the tide. And here, too, where water's
width greets the sky's November silence, the mind
may lose its anchor, may wind wearily into chaos,
become a coven of demons clutching at the body,
prowl frenetic for a voice to taunt broodingly at death.
Yet, whatever woos the tide inholds the water;
whatever guides the flight of geese over river,

wood and field permits also our demons to spit
defiance into their despair. Here is the Bay,
here the slow softly flow of river, the geese
in hectic scurry from a cloud-dooming sky;
and over there is death gnawing at discarded bone
under a leafless tree, trembling by bay-blue-wide
Susquehanna's ever placating stillness.

A Silver-Winged Seraph of Bonaventure*
Over Pennsylvania, USA

I
The stewardess gathers plastic cups
and peanut wrappers; an hour out
of Philadelphia and grey
Delaware's leaden flow behind.

An aircraft, become a Silver-
Winged Seraph, seems to hover
in this moment's stillness; from here,
and above, nothing is concealed

from the cold blue sun's sight: winding
rivers, lakes of winter's hoary
brown; russet-green fields bordered by
white highways, sheer-straight, horizon-
consumed.

II
Rain streaks across the window as
we descend through cloud. This return
is a communal journey on
our Winged Seraph, buffeted

by unseen winds; our bone of speech
heard; our marrow of grief heeded.
A found hunger throbs within me
this new desire for gracings, not

instruction. I ask from clay, not
clarity but the darkness; fire
aflame, not light; a furnace for
my soul's Jerusalem, groaning

in prayer, not the sun's hovering
cold above the Mississippi.
Sufficient, now, and here, a new
name written -- a mystery, silent
in sighs: *Bless the Lord... Let it be...*

---

*St Bonaventure (1221-1274), Doctor of the Church, mystic, teacher, and administrator; also known as the 'Seraphic Doctor'. The image of the 'Seraph' is taken from his mystical writings.

Canticle for Hosea
St. Louis Missouri, USA

I

I am an open wound, Yahweh,
here, among these grey tufted-tailed
squirrels scavenging in the bush,
skipping by paths where crickets sing
and cicadas hum into night.

Within the Sheol-pit of my
stomach there is only a numb
hunger for you, my Beloved,
the searing pain of loss, the cruel
mystery of tomorrow. Here, where

cicadas hum there is, now, no
consolation. You grant only
restless torment, demanding I
be your prophet of pain; here, where
crickets sing, I, an open wound.

II

Within the silence of Yahweh's
winter snow, I recall Fall leaves
aching to become flashing flames
as they dangled on tired trees sloped
into the wind. By the banks of
this green river, abandoned leaves
are my tears for you, Lo-rammi.

Now snows lie deep on pathways where
squirrels once skipped and scavenged. But
she would not be wooed in Yahweh's
brittle season, where silence is
a condemnation; memory
but a barren consolation.

III

Would that you would come into the
desert with me where cicadas
do not hum, where no crickets sing.
My breasts I gave you to suckle,
but you would not. When you were
my Desert People you wandered
in hope; by a green river you
secured only walls and condemned
me to these waiting expanses.

Only the sands heed me, the sun-
scorched rock knows a love-heat you knew
not. Your grief, my prophet, your tears,
have become mine. She lies beneath
the oak and poplar, my people
under pleasant shades; but I, a
lover's winter must endure.

Colleville-Sur-Mer, Normandy, France
American Military Cemetery

For once the set of a movie and reality
Seem the same – white-glinted marble
Crucifixes and Stars of David memorialize
As far as the eye can comprehend the waste,
The blind commitment to a rallying idea.

A group of teenage boys play, avoiding
Rugby tackles, dodging and weaving through
The mathematical intricacies of serried
Row upon row, until appalled and indignant
Stares quieten them to embarrassed bravado.

It is now dusk. Their names, gold-carved, turn grey
And ghost-fettered. I realise a strange reverence
Has stilled me to private tears for men deprived
Of the hurts and the hopes that we, daily, muddle through.

I-75 Florida Hurricane

Staying ahead of the hurricane
meant I had to drive through the pre-wake
of squalls and telegraph-tensing winds.

From the south it plundered on
through the swathe of grey blue horizon.
My destination overtaken, the rains sheeted

down the windscreen into a thick soup-fog;
hazard lights hardly registered and then
their blinking disappeared into nothing

and out of nothing reappeared again until
the nothing returned and the freeze-sweat fear
of being smashed from behind and thrown

into a something, any something in front
flung me into a limbo of panic where there
was no where and no destination ahead,

only now and the cataracting rain that kept
the outside world blind to me, and my hands
white-knuckle-tight on the steering wheel

muscle-squeezed my arms into terrorised
rigidity; then the windscreen cleared and
beheld a bonnet blue of sky, but the rear view

mirror swelled with that black-walled juggernaut.

Icescape
Perryvile, Maryland, USA

My mind is oblivious to the ingenious mechanics
of my body as I drive to work. It is occupied instead
with the daily common coil, the eternal problems:

return a phone call; remind myself to pay that bill.
Surely I was misunderstood. What was she really
trying to say to me? What chaos do we enter

when we enter ourselves? And what will befall,
should the Chaos come? I must, at least, remain in control;
if not, what pathways to the future will crumble beneath me?

Take a right turn here, my automatic pilot
takes over again as I drive through the familiar
tree-lined country road: undulating fields,

criss-crossed by low bush, new homes
under construction; lumber piles,
Tyvek insulation flapping tightly in the wind.

Last night winter must have wrapped her cocoon
with darkened mystery and opened just as dawn
edged the horizon; for I have come upon a crystal city,

a frozen ice-scape of shivering light, a shimmer
of sugar bush, musical spheres, white symphonies
of brittle silences, concertos of crinkled ice

echoing within the frigid earth, the white dusted
weeds, powdered fields and a blue Chevy truck
under a tree, ice-encrusted, seized by the winter grip.

Fearful am I of making a sound, even to breathe,
my throat constricted by the sweet shock of paralysis,
else it will all, all, shatter into pieces.

La Grotte - Lourdes

I
Bernadette under Massabielle

Massabiele that night overhung
The grey granite eye of Bernadette
Kneeling on gravel-bruised knees,
Staying the pain in anticipation.

If I were one crippled with palsy,
And my legs hung dangle-limp
Over a wheelchair, would I chew
The dirt-smirched weed to prove faith?

For hours you linger there,
The Gave gurgling south behind you,
And know; but afterwards
Would you trust your memory

To keep you during doubt's testing?
Perhaps our God is camouflaged in stone
Dumbness, and you, Bernadette,
Hanker into this rock cell,

Honing the flesh to an essential worship.

II
Return Journey (Doreen - In Memoriam)

The Arrivals Hall on the return journey
Has become the place we could not linger
Among trolleys heaped with baggage
And Lourdes Water bottles. A week
Before we shook hands gawkishly,
Now I embrace fearing loss
Among wheelchairs and Duty Free -- smiling

Through the scour of exhaustion. For you
And your suffering, and our minds
Nudging at the clutch of death, our tears
Have become bread broken to sorrow.
The Arrivals Hall ebbs and swells; the intercom
Dissonates through the throng of clutching spaces.

Leonard Cohen on Mt. Baldy, California, USA.

I

Imagine him, zen-stooped,
a brittle dawn belittled
by night, his Spanish guitar
silenced, as mantra, locus
of his engagement, each hour
cartographed with the minute
journeys of imagination.

Adobes of meditation
become the kiln of his song.

Seeped in tones of desperation
yet, though broken, its strings strum the
lineaments of the soul.
                            Image him,
Zen-stilled, longing his song through
another brittle dawn.

II

'The sick soul must be twice-born
To be happy', you quoted James.
For the sick soul perceives something there
As an objective, but unperceivable presence,
More real in the universe than what we can
Taste, touch, or fuck, something real
That mocks our beliefs, mocks the drugs
We ingest to silence it, mocks the applause
We seek to dissolve this bewildering
Anguish, this feeling of loss for what
We'll never possess.
                        And does the good
Doctor prescribe a cure for this malady?
Yes. The twice-born must experience
Religion, not as a dull habit, but
As an acute fever.
                        I was hoping he
Prescribed beautiful young women, you said.

Lines from Within Tintern Abbey, Monmouthshire, Wales.

He does not stand here in this ruin
of beauty and stone contemplating
nature and her all-encompassing spirit

while I listen to Spanish tourists
in gabble lilt organise a group
photo, Nikons, Canons and disposable

cameras strewn randomly on the
manicured patches of verge maintained
by the National Trust; he stands by the steep

slopes of Wye, her cataracts booming,
knelling his spirit to another
ruin nestled in the mind of those who long

to pilgrimage into a more deep seclusion,
restore the self to the service of Quietness.

To a Native American Standing by a Telegraph Post

Was it in a Kansas City Art Gallery
or in an American Art magazine,

within baroque gold framed,
there was he, standing in the white solitude,

within his own stillness, his left ear
leaning into a single telegraph post

listening?

And what could be deciphered,
what discerned through the staccato-

hummings from the stretched wires
above and ahead and behind,

the voices of the unyielding,
the machinators merely announcing

inevitabilities?

Mercer County
Maria Stein, Ohio, USA

I

The floor of Mercer County is soggy,
And wet it waits dry spring winds for sowing
After winter snows and rains have bogged in;

And in this place, where no seagulls glide, yet
Its clay in garden, flowerbed, harrowed field,
Wafts seaweed salt on a moist southern breeze.

Over cups of coffee we sit, apart,
Absorbing within our composed silence,
A self-fermenting soggy ground in sap,

Pondering bleak moments where origins
Will never be known except they emerge,
Pure gift, unexpected, in dumb sensing.

II

Hillocks not the height of a Chevy truck,
Nothing to break the wind, not hedge, nor ditch
But the gable end of a barn. A blight

Was souring potato fields in Ireland
When German farmers Leistenschneider, Gast,
Beckman bought, at a dollar an acre,

A churlish clay, yet biddable, a contour
For Teutonic precision; now you can walk
Five miles without a bend on the road

By fields yet to be sown in bean and corn -
Contours of the self resist such logic -
Back Home we furrow when landscape allows.

III

After rain the robin prances, a prince
Among trout lilies; the garden aflame
With red-breasted dignity; in a sunken

Wheel-track of trapped rain another bathes, wing
Clapping his delight; we are shy with them

When we come upon them from our moments

Of solitude; a fear of intrusion:
For each snap of stick that scares them to flight,
Or each unquiet, unheeded movement

Shatters a fragile attunement. Could there
Be a time when we might sit with them -
A sort of consonance among creatures?

IV
This landscape: farm houses, barns, harvest towers,
Tree clumps, islands in a sea of harrowed
Fields; a mile is what your eye can decide

Between one horizon and another.
And on stilly, cloud-washed evenings, the coo-
ing of the mourning dove from nearby woods

Is an unfulfilled echo from the past,
Resonating with my haunted inner
Landscape: a clump of anger is tracing

Itself backwards to a clutching regret
Which echoes from beyond horizons where
Woods are islands, forever out of reach.

Mourning Dove
Maria Stein, Ohio, USA

I
In this heat hangs that throaty tang only
Cow-dung heaviness gives; tractors are out
Ranging the fields with manure. Mourning doves

Have flown in, all swoop and savvy; all this
Is elemental: breaking open the sod,
The harrowing, the preparing of clay

For the seed. Farming is this tending clay,
Plumbing the smells and stirrings in the earth,
Where brow-sweat precedes an awakening;

A time for what Rilke calls 'heart-work':
When our sensings become clay; when doves
Return to build again precarious nests.

II
As you face the front from the avenue
The roof is low, wind deflecting; the drain
Pipe at the bend just below the eaves holds

A mourning dove's brown nest, tucked in. She's been
Sitting in that nest for at least a week,
Waiting; her grey head with black bill and eye

Ever guarding. The wind which blew in from
The warm south has changed, and now blows north-east,
Which means it blows face on into her nest.

But there's more than waiting, there's the brooding,
There's the attending to the slow soft pulse
Thickening inside walls of porcelain blue.

III
To keep returning as I do each day
Checking on the mourning dove in her nest,
I must be tending myself. Do I wait

As she? What would happen if some freakish
Wind blew her nest, her eggs destroyed? Return

To picking grubs in the clay, another

One of galaxies' games? Perhaps these are
The inevitabilities. But Habakkuk says:
'If it seems to tarry wait for it...' Was

This a prayer of hope out of hopelessness,
Or trust in the pulse of the universe,
Beseeching a vigil of readiness?

IV
The shoulder on this part of the earth
Glistens with the dew of its sweat and tears;
It is morning and the sun romps

A myriad jig on the haze of seeding fields;
A breeze skims the pond water
Disturbing nothing of what scurries beneath;

The earth shakes unfelt in a rumble where
Burrow holes lie by trunks of fallen trees.
That mourning dove pecks at grubs in the lawn

While her two chicks wait in her ragged nest;
What growings there be in darkness
Are flouncing in the sun's sight.

Notre Dame, Paris

The tour guide pointed to Notre Dame
on the left, all gargoyles, buttresses

and saints carved with medieval
naiveté. "They used it as a warehouse

for storing grain and food during
the Revolution, and for many years

after..." A thousand years Daughter
of the Church loathed to such an act

of rejection. The Christ of the Bishops
of Paris rebuked the people from marble

pulpits, while He, unnoticed, tended to horses
and fed them grain there. On the Rue

St. Denis a desolating aristocracy shambled
to their chateaux caring nothing for either.

Post Cards from Berlin

I

The U2 to Olympia Stadion.

A pair of granite horse-tamers
face the Langmarckehalle
flanking the western entrance.

In art is myth so ensouled:
a bell tower sounds to the
selfless sacrifice of youth,

horse-tamers to subordination
of the soul to the state. But
the order of the unified heart

embraces brokenness where
the only subordination
is to the care of the other.

II

The U2 to Alexanderplatz

Post-war concrete and glass
have replaced the splendour
of baroque statehouses.

In Mariankirche, nails from
Coventry Cathedral have been
presented – 'Father forgive them'

is enscribed on a brass plate;
from a lonely tower
only the broken dare forgive.

Sisters of Charity – Leavenworth, Kansas, USA

Wheelchair rubber squeaks on parquet
floors; a farmhouse of green gables
can be spied through the January
silence of trees. We sit together
for the Eucharist celebrated

as wheelchairs take their places. These
infirm women greet old age with
gentleness or silent rage, their
faith denying meaningless
existence, their lives spent as signs

that God has hands and compassionate
eyes. The Founders in their time dreamed
their risks. Did she, by the Missouri,
as her crates were counted, dream these
buildings, this room, this Eucharist as

a prayer of her dying and their
impending death? Their work is done.
God is being revealed beyond this
room. This Eucharist precedes all dreams
risked into spring.

Therese Martin
Lisieux, France

Traveling through France, we were
thirteen in a minibus, packed elbow
on shoulder, panting for the next

stretch-leg stop. Our baggage and tents
tied down by tarpaulin and it
flapping into a mainsail, bedragging

us into the bracing crosswind, down
the morning motorway to Lisieux.
After *Coke* and those foul-smelling *Gauloises,*

we took the required photographs
of your basilica -- a white meringue
of spires -- and had till three to browse

through souvenirs, and eat maybe a green
peppered pizza, or a twenty franc *jambon
sandwich,* its crusty flakes crumbling

into a saucered hand. I wandered
downhill to the medieval cathedral:
outside, a speckle-mossed buttress wall, but

inside the summer light was pale, almost
mist-delicate; and I sat where you sat,
the floor there stone-buckled, dusting

into a film of sand. Your white statue
pencil marked, seeking favours -- appealing
to a child. I thought of your waterfall

blonde hair twisted into a bride-knot,
and young men gazing after you, as you
carry a basket of green apples home.

The 'Scaffetta'
Venice, Italy

In the shelf-hole of the wall at the
Ospedale della Pieta, in the lagooned

city of mendacious masks, four baby
girls per day are pushed through;

Marina, five days old, wrapped in rat
stained rags; Agata, in Venetian silk,

red woolen leggings, trimmed with
Burano lace, as noted in bureaucratic

jaded pen: *'one finger on her left hand,
one toe on her left foot, and on her right*

three toes'; disfigured and unwanted,
where brutalising poverty has condemned

them, or are un-contractable in the market
of pre-arranged husbands; but tourists come,

their disfigurement hidden behind a grille
in the gallery, where they sing and play

a music of angelic purity, eroticised to a
fantasy of loveliness, while the papal curse,

carved upon a stone slab on the wall,
excoriates their abandonment;

their lives commodified through
the *scaffetta's* exculpatory pit.

Viola da Gamba of Kyiv

Is there in Kyiv a viola da gamba playing now?
This creation of Andreas Amati of Cremona.
Its high arch and wide purfling of pear wood
and poplar, elegantly curved scrolls and body

conceived around an arrangement of concentric
circles, all shaped to a harmony of geometry
and the harmony of contemplative sound?

Or has it been silenced and smashed to pieces
by the bombs of the Kremlin Mad Man,
its luthier dead, exiled, or recruited?

Its only hope is his return, so the carvings
and inlays, its golden maplewood and
four strings, will be tuned once again to
bow the quadrille of dance and elegance.

Welsh Speakers in Trafalgar Square

They never achieved independence of soil
or geography, a principality of the
colonist and conqueror, yet they speak
an independent tongue, not in defiance
as we, but to converse of ordinary jack of

all day things like the two women in
Trafalgar Square calling over their friend
to where they are sitting, and he comes,
greeting them as if he came upon them
sitting on a gate gazing out into the valleys.

We Speak the Same Language
Bugibba Square, Malta

He comes each day and sits on the bench
beside her as he has done ever since
he moved here from Scotland. She knows
his habits and has been expecting him.

"They're building an hotel next door."
"Aye, I heard."
"And an apartment block on the other side."
"Aye, I heard."

"Cuts off my sun in the morning and I only
get an hour or so depending on the weather."
"Aye, I heard."

"It's terrible what they are doing. They don't care."
"Aye. It's the same everywhere. Money. Profit.
That's all they care about."
"Aye."

The Square faces the island where Paul
was shipwrecked on his way to Rome.
He, too, might have sat here on a November
evening and heard such conversations
that while the day away to simple quietness.

"I'm going home now."
"What'll you do?"
"I'll buy some bread and cheese, read, watch TV. You?"
"I'll stay until five or so. It gets dark early now."

Winter - Fort de Soto, Florida

Sea terns hunt by white beach edges.
Swept steadily by gulf winds, they
pitch and turn for the kill in a wing
flutter of hovering poise; judge carefully

their stuka-dive abandonment of flight,
as they climb again and again out of the grey sea,
ever flapping across winter's pale sky,
hunting sea morsels into sunset.

I wonder at this site Lee had chosen
to defend the bay, a Spanish discovery,
once a US Army fort camouflaged
among sand dunes and sentried palms,

and shiver at reflection -- what soldier
would have desired an outpost of mosquitos,
summer's sticky sweat and winter's long
loneliness? This, once, must have been

a station of demotion, perhaps a military
punishment, a banishment to the continent's
edge. I guess these great guns were never
shot in anger. What enemy ever attacked,

ever sailed into these waters? And what rituals
had they conjured to mark time and occasions
besides their endless military drill? Cocktails
in the officer's mess; baseball perhaps? And

the wife, waiting for the weekly mail,
the Sears-Roebuck, a new hat, a letter
from home. Did she crave her husband's
promotion; or wait with carefully calibrated

patience a transfer by dint of seniority? But
at sunset, in white linen, she too, as she swept
the endless blowings of gulf sand, must have
watched in a moment of quiet poise,

sea terns hunt by white beach edges.

Zambian Diptych

I

By the smoky grass huts of Mangango
through the deep green sleep of bush
we drive over hill after hill of orange
dirt-track, rattling and bouncing in a rust-pocked

Land Rover; a gush-swirl of dust trails behind.
With a snatch of tribal dance, gaggling
children run to greet us, hallooing:
"Aii makua! Aii makua!" waving

their flag-a-flutter hands after us. I keep
remembering journeys into the bog-expanse
of Erris and the road to Ballyhaunis rising
and dipping, and an old man walking

with his bicycle, nodding at us as if
we were his next door neighbour. But now
we drive past a farmer droving his cow,
its arched horns menacing the sky.

II

By the river Zambesi
red poinsettias bloom
ballet-poised on wiry stems
flames of dying sun.

A freight of twig-heaped firewood
is upstream paddled
to Lukulu, where melon-huge
paw-paw fruit grows, as green-drenched

as the meadows of County Meath.
On a path of grey-sooted sand
a mother and her child,
cloth-bound to aching back,

balances on her head
a basin of cassava root
returning to her village
where useless hens peck and grub

under the sun-sheltering
cha-ka cha-ka tree;
her sterile soil
is Kalahari blown

smothering her field
from year to year
-- a silent *banshee*
of destruction.

Afterword

The location and time of one's birth, of one's experience of early, middle and late childhood; the location and time of one's dawning awareness of self; the places where we experience the smell, touch and sight of our personal environment is key to the life of the person.

It determines identity, tribal affiliation, family connections, cultural influences and formation; it locates the unique experiences that form the structure of a person's being and becoming.

The geographical landscape, the fields, rivers, canals, and various waterways; the hills, glens, mountains, woods, forests; the suburban and cityscapes, whether at home or abroad, as well as the family living spaces, are never forgotten, never truly unconscious in the day to day unfolding of the mind and sensual experiences of the body, the spiritual and religious life, the internal and external worlds, of the individual.

What marks the individual is the conscious capability of being able to connect to a sense of place, and being able to locate and root oneself to the centrality of existence; the reality of one's personal and unique experience of place provides the borders of experience and the boundaries of movement that can be both a security for, and a stifling of, one's personality.

This collection of poems, **The Geography of Feeling**, explores the poet's own personal locations, places and spaces that have been the root of his experiences. They may be unique and individual, but they enable the reader to tap into their own geography of feeling, their emotional and intellectual life, and thus has a universal relevance to the reader of poetry.

A note on the layout and sequence of poems:

There are two parts in this collection. Part One contain poems set in Ireland, and Part Two are poems set in places outside Ireland.

I have arranged the collection alphabetically by title. It may seem arbitrary but it may be reflecting the arbitrary nature of life.

Acknowledgements

Thanks to Sean Ruane, Paul O'Leary, Clare O'Reilly as well as the Inklings Writer's Group Mullingar for all their support and encouragement.

Page 14: The last line is a quotation from Keats' Ode on Melancholy, Stanza II.

Page 76, Part II of Leonard Cohen on Mt. Baldy, California, USA., is based on a conversation between Leonard Cohen and Eric Lerner, in Lerner's Matters of Vital Interest, 2018, Da Capo Press.